**Best Selling Series
CONSOLIDATION EXERCISES
PHOTOCOPIABLE
MASTERS**

Level 1

Spelling Made *Easy*

Consolidation Exercises For Spelling Made Easy
Level 1 Text Book

by
Violet Brand and Katy Brand

Fun with Phonics
Consolidation Exercises
for
Spelling Made Easy Level One
First published in the United Kingdom in 2005
by Violet and Katy Brand

Digs and Bangs by Violet Brand

Copyright assigned to BrandBooks
(a division of G & M Brand Publications Ltd) Violet Brand and Katy Brand (2005)

ISBN 1-904421 156

All rights reserved. The copymasters contained in this publication are protected by international copyright laws. The copyright of all materials in the 'Spelling Made Easy' series remains the property of the publisher and the author. The publisher hereby grants photocopying rights of this work for use with 'Spelling Made Easy' textbooks. Otherwise, no part of this book may be reproduced or translated in any form or by any means, electronic or mechanical, including recording or by any information storage or retrieval system without permission in writing from the publisher.

Illustrated by Adam Pickering

CONTENTS

Fun with Phonics
Level One

Introduction

Exercises	page	Answers page
1. Short vowel sounds a,o,e,i,u	2,3	42
2. Short vowel sounds a,o,e,i,u	4,5	43
3. Vowel Blending and Consonant Clusters ck,ee,oo,ar,or	6,7	44
4. Vowel Blending and Consonant Clusters ck,ee,oo,ar,or	8,9	45
5. Consonant Clusters and Magic 'e' sh,ch,th,a-e,i-e	10,11	46
6. Consonant Clusters and Magic 'e' sh,ch,th,a-e,i-e	12,13	47
7. Vowel Blending and Magic 'e' o-e,u-e,ai,oa,ir	14,15	48
8. Vowel Blending and Magic 'e' o-e,u-e,ai,oa,ir	16,17	49
9. Vowel Blending and Endings ou,ea,ay,ing,ur	18,19	50
10. Vowel Blending and Endings ou,ea,ay,ing,ur	20,21	51
11. Vowel Blending and Endings aw,oi,all,er,ea	22,23	52
12. Vowel Blending and Endings aw,oi,all,er,ea	24,25	53
13. Various ow,igh,a,o,y	26,27	54
14. Various ow,igh,a,o,y	28,29	55
15. Various ow,ew,tion,au,i,oy	30,31	56
16. Various ow,ew,tion,au,i,oy	32,33	57

(continued)

Contents (Continued)

Exercises	page	Answers page
17. Various ear, ai, ou, a, ph	34, 35	58
18. Various ear, ai, ou, a, ph	36, 37	59
19. Various o, are, ough, ar	38, 39	60
20. Various o, are, ough, ar	40, 41	61
Digs and Bangs (Story)		62

INTRODUCTION

BrandBooks is delighted to bring you Fun With Phonics, a series of consolidation exercises to perfectly complement the rest of Violet Brand's best-selling Spelling Made Easy series. Fun With Phonics comprises a set of four workbooks, colour-coded to match each of the existing textbooks and worksheet books.

Each Fun With Phonics book is fully photocopiable and designed to be used in conjunction with its corresponding textbook. Each book takes between two and five of the word families found in the textbook and provides four pages of interesting and stimulating exercises, including passages for reading aloud, reading comprehension tests, word searches, crosswords and much more.

Each series of exercises is based on a continuous story featuring Sam and Jim, the well-known characters from the textbooks. In many cases pupils will not recognise that they are being tested and that basic skills are being reinforced. Field tests have shown that pupils simply enjoy them. They are designed to put the fun into phonics!

Finally, Violet Brand has produced a new Sam story, which can be found at the back of the book. This is not tied specifically to the textbooks but is suitable for pupils who have reached the end of the Level One (Green) book. This can be reproduced and read as homework or for pure enjoyment to bring confidence to readers.

The 'Spelling Made Easy' series was conceived, written and published at a time when teaching reading and spelling though phonics was out of fashion in the UK, as were multi sensory techniques.

After publication in 1984 the textbook series was quickly recognized as highly effective and it continues to be widely used and purchased by primary and special schools in the UK and their equivalents in other parts of the world where English is taught.

Violet Brand was awarded the MBE for services to literacy, and has always believed that literacy skills must be taught in a way that is both relevant and fun in order to become a tool for life.

"Spelling in isolation is not enough. The word building skills acquired must be integrated into literacy generally. For a few children this will happen automatically, but for others, tasks which will gently edge them along the path will be essential. Constant reinforcement will be necessary."

– Violet Brand MBE

1. Short Vowel Sounds
'a', 'o', 'e', 'i', 'u'

**Spelling Made Easy
Level 1 Textbook
Pages 10 – 14**

1a Reading Exercise

Sam has a pal. The pal is a tramp. Sam and the tramp will camp in a tent, next to a pond. On the trip Sam and the tramp will have a picnic. Sam has the picnic in a string bag. Sam has crisps and a mint drink in the bag. The tramp has a drum. At sunset he will bang his drum. Sam's dog will go with the two men. The dog can smell the crisps in the bag. He cannot get them, as the bag is strong. Sam, the tramp and the dog get to the pond. Sam dumps the tent and scrubs his hands. The tramp rips the bag of crisps and lets the dog have a sniff.

1b Reading Comprehension

Use the story to help fill in the gaps:

Sam has a _____.
Sam will camp in a _____.
Sam and the tramp will camp next to a _____.
Sam has a picnic in a _____ bag.
The tramp will bang his _____.
Sam's _____ will go with the men.
The dog can _____ the crisps in the bag.
Sam _____ his hands.
The tramp rips the _____ of crisps.
He lets the dog have a _____.

1c Write the correct word underneath each picture.

  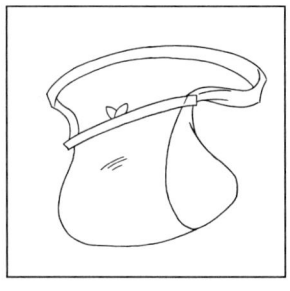

_____   _____   _____

_____   _____

1d Wordsearch

There are 10 words from the story hidden in the box below. They **only** go from left to right.

t	r	a	m	p	q	w	t	m	o
a	p	o	n	d	m	j	l	k	p
v	f	g	y	u	s	n	i	f	f
s	m	e	l	l	e	z	u	i	p
z	x	f	d	r	u	m	t	y	n
s	t	r	o	n	g	r	g	b	m
q	t	m	a	b	a	n	g	c	k
n	o	y	h	m	n	e	x	t	l
s	c	r	u	b	d	w	m	e	r
m	f	p	i	c	n	i	c	h	j

1e Wordmuddle

Write the words below next to the correct letter. Some of the words do not appear in the story.

hand   smell   king   scrub   cost
drink   dog   bank   desk   plug

a _____ _____   o _____ _____

e _____ _____   u _____ _____

i _____ _____

1f Choose your favourite part of the story. On a separate sheet of paper, draw a picture of it and write a sentence underneath it. Colour in your picture.

2. Short Vowel Sounds
'a', 'o', 'e', 'i', 'u'

**Spelling Made Easy
Level 1 Textbook
Pages 10 – 14**

2a Reading Exercise

Sam and the tramp are on a trip. Sam must put up his tent. He has one canvas and a hundred pegs. Sam thinks he will have his crisps and his mint drink. He sits next to the tramp and the dog. He pops the top off his drink and rips his bag of crisps. Sam and the tramp have the picnic next to the pond at sunset. Sam has had his crisps. Sam gets up. He puts up the tent, but the tramp will not help! The tramp just bangs his drum. The dog gets the rest of the crisps. A frog jumps up from the pond and sits on the drum.

2b Use the story to help fill in the gaps:

Sam and the _____ are on a trip.
Sam _____ put up the tent.
Sam has one _____.
Sam has a _____ pegs.
Sam will have his _____ drink.
He sits _____ to the tramp.
Sam and the tramp have their picnic next to the _____.
The dog gets the _____ of the crisps.
A _____ jumps up from the pond.
The frog _____ on the drum.

2c Picture

There are 5 words from the story in the picture below. Write the correct words underneath the box.

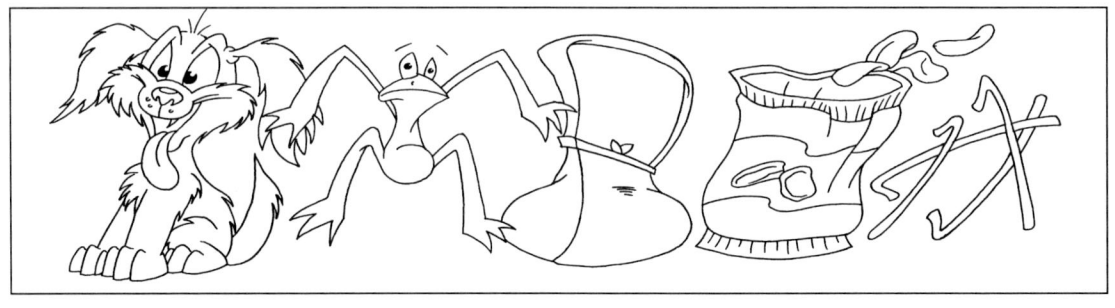

_____ _____ _____ _____ _____

2d Crossword

Use the clues and the story to solve the crossword puzzle.

Across
1. Sam has a mint ____. (5)
2. Sam's pal. (5)
3. Sits in a pond and jumps up. (4)

Down
1. Sam camps next to a ____. (4)
2. Sam must put it up. (4)
3. The tramp will bang it. (4)
4. Pins the tent. (4)
5. Carry things in it. (3)

2e Wordsorting

Below are 10 new words. Write them next to the correct letter.

scrap   left   sting   lump   frost
ring   drop   sprang   yell   bunk

a _____ _____   o _____ _____

e _____ _____   u _____ _____

i _____ _____

2f On a separate sheet of paper draw a picture of Sam trying to put up the tent, and the tramp sitting down and banging his drum. Colour it in and write a sentence underneath to describe the picture.

3. Vowel Blending and Consonant Clusters
'ck', 'ee', 'oo', 'ar', 'or'

Spelling Made Easy
Level 1 Textbook
Pages 15 - 19

3a Reading Exercise

Sam puts up the tent. He must be quick as it is dark. Sam, the tramp and the dog will sleep in the tent. If Sam cannot put the tent up, they will have to sleep in the wood. The wood is next to the pond. A frog jumps onto Sam's arm. Sam jumps back and drops the tent pegs. Just then, a duck steps up from the pond. The duck starts to peck Sam's heel. Sam can see forty ducks on the pond. The tramp sits on a stool and bangs his drum. A bee stings Sam's leg and the dog starts to bark. Soon it will be morning and the tent is still not up!

3b Reading Comprehension

Use the story to help fill in the gaps:

Sam must be _____ as it is dark.
Sam, the tramp and the dog will _____ in the tent.
The _____ is next to the pond.
A frog jumps onto Sam's _____.
A _____ steps up from the pond.
It starts to peck Sam's _____.
Sam can see _____ ducks on the pond.
The tramp sits on a _____.
The dog starts to _____.
Soon it will be _____.

3c Pictures

Use the story and the pictures to fill in the gaps.

A frog jumps onto Sam's _____.

The _____ pecks Sam's _____.

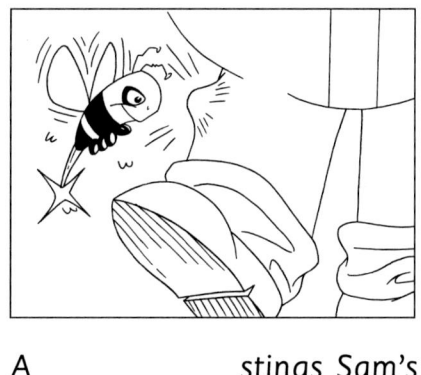

A _____ stings Sam's leg.

The _____ is next to the pond.

3c Wordsearch

There are 10 words hidden in the square below. They **only** go from left to right.

q	u	i	c	k	m	p	z	a	r
d	f	g	m	y	s	t	a	r	t
t	n	s	o	o	n	k	l	u	f
c	b	a	r	k	v	m	b	k	d
x	v	b	f	o	r	t	y	m	l
b	w	f	t	m	s	l	e	e	p
a	m	o	r	n	i	n	g	i	o
f	v	w	o	o	d	u	m	j	k
s	e	e	f	y	t	r	s	x	m
m	o	k	l	g	d	d	u	c	k

3d Wordmuddle

Write the words below next to the correct letter group. Some of the words do not appear in the story.

    peck   car   need   bark   pool
    heel   wood   born   clock   forty

ck _____ _____   or _____ _____

ee _____ _____   ar _____ _____

oo _____ _____

3e On a separate sheet of paper draw a picture of the frog on Sam's arm. Colour it in and write a sentence underneath to describe it.

4. Vowel Blending and Consonant Clusters
'ck', 'ee', 'oo', 'ar', 'or'

**Spelling Made Easy
Level 1 Textbook
Pages 15 – 19**

4a Reading Exercise

Sam needs help! The tramp sees the duck peck Sam's heel, the frog on his arm and the bee sting his leg. Sam's leg starts to smart. The tramp drops his drum and runs to help. The tramp picks up the tent pegs and claps his hands. He bangs his boots hard. The duck runs back into the pond. The frog jumps into the wood. Sam picks up the canvas. He sees that it is torn. There is a big gap in the roof of the tent! It is morning and the sun is up. Sam and the tramp have had no sleep. It is not a good start to the trip! Sam and the tramp have a quick snack. They must not be greedy for they need to mend the tent.

4b Reading Comprehension

Use the story to fill in the gaps:

Sam _____ help!
The frog is on Sam's _____.
Sam's leg starts to _____.
The tramp bangs his _____ hard.
The duck runs _____ into the pond.
Sam sees that the canvas is _____.
It is not a _____ start to the trip!
Sam and the tramp have a quick _____.
They must not be _____.
They must not be greedy _____ they need to mend the tent.

4c Pictures

Draw pictures of the words that appear underneath each box.

bee	duck	boot

4d Crossword

Use the clues and the story to fill in the crossword.

Across
1. Put on your feet if it is wet. (5)
2. A quick bite. (5)
3. Back of the foot (4)

Down
1. Not bad! (4)
2. To begin (5)
3. The duck does this to Sam. (4)
4. Do this in bed. (5)

4e Wordsorting

Below are 10 new words. Write them next to the correct letter group.

farm   broom   queen   story   trick
seed   luck   look   garden   more

ck _____ _____   oo _____ _____

ee _____ _____   or _____ _____

ar _____ _____

4f Choose your favourite part of the story. On a separate sheet of paper, draw a picture of it and write a sentence underneath. Colour in your picture.

5. Consonant Clusters and Magic 'e'
'sh', 'ch', 'th', 'a-e', 'i-e'

**Spelling Made Easy
Level 1 Textbook
Pages 20 - 24**

5a Reading Exercise

Sam and the tramp drop the tent. The tramp's name is Gus. Gus blames Sam for the fact that he has had no sleep. Sam tells Gus that he was no help with the tent. Sam and Gus have lunch. For lunch, Sam has chicken and chips. Gus has a fish pie. Sam likes the taste of chicken and chips. Gus gets fish pie on his face. They sit on a bench next to the pond. A thrush starts to sing. This makes Sam and Gus smile. The sun is hot. Sam and Gus cool off in the pond. They rush in and make a big splash. It is nice and cool in the pond. Sam makes a ship from twigs and a sheet of cloth.

5b Reading Comprehension

Use the story to help fill in the gaps:

The tramp's _____ is Gus.
Gus _____ Sam for the fact that he has had no sleep.
Sam and Gus have _____.
Sam has _____ and chips.
Sam _____ the taste of chicken.
A _____ starts to sing.
They rush into the pond and make a big _____.
It is _____ and cool in the pond.
Sam makes a _____ from twigs and a sheet of _____.

5c Pictures

Write the correct word underneath each picture.

_____   _____

5d Wordsearch

There are 10 words from the story hidden in the box below. They go from left to right **AND** top to bottom.

t	h	e	y	t	r	m	n	l	n
m	s	h	e	e	t	j	t	i	a
f	g	h	j	v	m	a	a	l	m
b	e	n	c	h	u	y	s	v	e
z	s	m	i	l	e	y	t	r	b
x	q	f	b	n	c	g	e	p	v
n	i	c	e	g	l	p	j	m	s
b	m	o	k	l	o	d	s	c	h
j	k	p	t	m	t	e	f	x	i
c	h	i	p	s	h	d	m	b	p

5e Wordmuddle

Write the words below next to the correct letter group. Some of the words do not appear in the story.

    ship   cloth   chips   thud   taste
    ride   came   smile   rush   such

sh _____ _____   a-e _____ _____

ch _____ _____   i-e _____ _____

th _____ _____

5f On a separate sheet of paper, draw a picture of Sam and Gus in the pond. Draw some animals in the pond and label them. Colour in your picture.

6. Consonant Clusters and Magic 'e'
   'sh', 'ch', 'th', 'a-e', 'i-e'

Spelling Made Easy
Level 1 Textbook
Pages 20 - 24

6a Reading Exercise

Sam and Gus are in the pond. The dog runs in too. He jumps onto Sam's chest with a big crash. It makes such a splash and lots of froth! Gus slides on the mud in the pond. He hits his cheek on the dog's leg. Sam, Gus and the dog get onto the bank. Sam rubs the dog with a cloth. The dog shakes and Sam and Gus lie in the hot sun. It is nice for them. Sam and Gus have a good long sleep. When they wake it is dark and they still have no tent. They are five miles from Sam's car. The wood next to the pond is dark. Gus does not like the dark.

6b Reading Comprehension

Use the story to help fill in the gaps:

The dog jumps onto Sam's _____ with a big _____.
It makes such a _____ and lots of _____.
Gus _____ on the mud in the pond.
Gus hits his _____ on the dog's leg.
Sam rubs the dog with a _____.
The dog _____.
Sam and Gus _____ in the hot sun.
When they _____ it is dark.
_____ still have no tent.

6c Picture

In the picture below are four words from the story. Write the correct words underneath the box.

_____   _____   _____   _____

6d Crossword

Use the clues and the story to fill in the crossword:

Across
1. On the sides of your face. (6)
2. A big bang. (5)
3. Mix it up. (5)
4. 1, 2, 3, 4, ___, 6, 7. (4)

Down
1. Wipe up a mess with it. (5)
2. Your ribs are inside this. (5)
3. We like you if you act like this. (4)
4. Get up in the morning. (4)

6e Wordsorting

Below are 10 new words. Write them next to the correct letter group.

| tie | chop | thing | cash | drive |
| came | shot | wave | crunch | moth |

sh _____ _____   a-e _____ _____

ch _____ _____   i-e _____ _____

th _____ _____

6f Choose your favourite part of the story. On a separate sheet of paper, draw a picture of it and write a sentence underneath. Colour in your picture.

7. Vowel Blending and Magic 'e'
'o-e', 'u-e', 'ai', 'oa', 'ir'

Spelling Made Easy
Level 1 Textbook
Pages 25 - 29

7a Reading Exercise

Sam and Gus are alone in the dark wood. They have no tent. They are far from home and have no phone. It starts to rain. Sam and Gus have no coats. Gus starts to moan. They run to a big fir tree in the wood to hide from the rain. They had just dried off from the pond and the rain has made them wet again! It is not good to have rain in June. The rain wakes up the toads and the snails in the wood. Sam hates toads and snails. Gus likes them. He picks a toad up. It is dirty. Sam thinks he will faint. His face is blue. Gus had no clue that Sam is afraid of toads. The dog is thirsty.

7b Reading Comprehension

Use the story to help fill in the gaps:

Sam and Gus are _____ in the dark wood.
They are far from _____.
It starts to _____.
Sam and Gus have no _____.
They run to a big _____ tree.
The rain has made them wet _____.
It is not good to have rain in _____.
Sam hates _____ and snails.
Gus had no _____ that Sam is afraid of toads.
The dog is _____.

7c Pictures

Use the story and the pictures to fill in the gaps.

Sam and Gus are far from _____ and have no _____.

Sam and Gus run to a big _____ tree to hide from the _____.

Sam hates _____ and _____.

Gus had no _____ that Sam hates toads.

7d Wordsearch

There are 10 words from the story hidden in the box below. They go from left to right **AND** top to bottom.

d	i	r	t	y	r	y	n	f	k
s	d	b	p	h	o	n	e	a	e
f	m	c	u	m	o	a	n	i	m
v	a	o	f	e	x	t	z	n	t
j	x	a	g	s	h	j	m	t	h
u	c	t	m	i	m	y	g	k	i
n	v	s	a	g	a	i	n	m	r
e	b	m	z	t	g	n	d	a	s
m	j	b	l	u	e	u	l	j	t
g	a	l	o	n	e	m	f	p	y

7e Wordmuddle

Write the words below next to the correct letter group. Some of the words do not appear in the story.

coat home girl nail blue
afraid clue roast rose thirsty

o-e _____ _____   ir _____ _____

u-e _____ _____   ai _____ _____

oa _____ _____

7f On a separate sheet of paper, draw a picture of Gus holding a toad and a snail and Sam going blue. Write a sentence underneath the picture and colour it in.

8. Vowel Blending and Magic 'e'
  'o-e', 'u-e', 'ai', 'oa', 'ir'

Spelling Made Easy
Level 1 Textbook
Pages 25 – 29

8a Reading Exercise

Gus must revive Sam. He gets his flute and makes a tune. But it is no use. The dog licks Sam's face. Sam blinks and sits up. Gus smiles but Sam groans. He is thirsty and dirty. He has a pain in his nose. Sam's wish is to be in his bed at home, not in the rain with Gus. There are loads of toads. They look like stones. They are so close to Sam and he hates it. Sam does not wait for Gus to pick a toad up again. He gets up and runs from the toads. Gus runs too. They end up next to a big oak tree in the wood. They have no clue where they can be. There are thirty tracks into the woods. They are lost and Gus is afraid. There is no hope.

8b Reading Comprehension

Use the story to fill in the gaps:

Gus gets his _____ and makes a tune.
Gus smiles, but Sam _____.
Sam is thirsty and _____.
Sam has a _____ in his nose.
Sam's wish is to be in his bed at _____.
There are _____ of toads.
They look like _____.
They have no _____ where they can be.
There are _____ tracks into the woods.
They are lost and Gus is _____.

8c Picture

Draw a picture in each box of the word that appears underneath.

toad	dirty	nose

8d Crossword

Use the clues and the story to fill in the crossword:

Across
1. A moan (5)
2. In need of a drink. (7)
3. You feel this if you crack a bone. (4)

Down
1. Are you _____ of monsters? (6)
2. Hum it or sing it. (4)
3. You feel this if you make a wish. (4)
4. A rock. (5)
5. This is what you will be if you jump in the mud. (5)

8e Wordsorting

Below are 10 new words. Write them next to the correct letter group.

| note | glue | soak | sail | close |
| girl | paint | stir | true | coal |

ai _____ _____   o-e _____ _____

oa _____ _____   u-e _____ _____

ir _____ _____

8f Choose your favourite part of the story. On a sheet of paper, draw a picture and write a sentence to describe it. Colour in your picture.

9. Vowel Blending and Endings
'ou', 'ea', 'ay', 'ing', 'ur'

**Spelling Made Easy
Level 1 Textbook
Pages 30 - 35**

9a Reading Exercise

Sam and Gus are lost in the wood and it is raining hard. Having got to the pond on Thursday, Sam tells Gus that the next day will be Saturday! Taking Sam's arm, Gus smiles and says that they may be under the tree until next Wednesday. Hoping that Gus is just joking, Sam starts to shout out for help. The dog runs up at the sound of Sam shouting. Its fur is wet from the rain. It digs in the ground and gets a turnip. Sam wants to get back to his house. He is dreaming of peach ice-cream. The dog is dreaming of a bed of hay. Gus just wants a cup of tea. There is a sound from the oak tree. Sam and Gus look up. They see a wet cat is stuck.

9b Reading Comprehension

Use the story to help fill in the gaps:

Sam tells Gus that the next _____ will be Saturday.
Gus smiles and says they _____ be under the tree until next Wednesday.
_____ that Gus is just _____, Sam shouts for help.
The dog runs up at the _____ of Sam shouting.
The dog's _____ is wet from the rain.
Sam wants to get back to his _____.
The dog digs up a _____.
Sam is dreaming of _____ ice-cream.
Gus just wants a cup of _____.

9c Pictures

Write the correct word underneath each picture.

_____   _____   _____

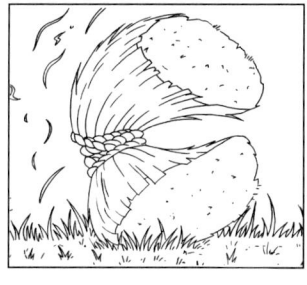   

_____   _____

9d Wordsearch

There are 10 words from the story hidden in the box. They only go from left to right.

m	s	f	h	j	y	u	m	a	y
c	r	e	a	m	r	t	v	d	a
g	h	k	l	t	a	k	i	n	g
z	v	t	m	s	o	u	n	d	m
j	o	k	i	n	g	x	c	h	f
w	m	o	h	a	y	p	f	d	r
t	h	u	r	s	d	a	y	m	t
y	s	h	o	u	t	u	e	c	v
x	c	m	d	f	g	h	t	e	a
f	u	r	z	y	x	m	g	j	u

9e Wordmuddle

Write the words below next to the correct letter group. Some of the words do not appear in the story.

    house   tray   mouth   please   fur
    sliding   tea   church   hoping   may

ou _____ _____   ay _____ _____

ea _____ _____   ur _____ _____

ing _____ _____

9f On a separate sheet of paper, draw a picture of Sam, Gus and the dog under the oak tree, looking up at the stray cat. Write a sentence to describe it and colour in the picture.

10. Vowel Blending and Endings
   'ou', 'ea', 'ay', ing', 'ur'

**Spelling Made Easy
Level 1 Textbook
Pages 30 - 35**

10a Reading Exercise

Gus says to Sam that they must rescue the stray cat. The dog jumps about and barks. The cat curls around the tree trunk. The cat does not like the dog. Sam tells Gus to close his mouth and not make a sound. Sam leaps onto the tree trunk and starts making his way up. He gets to the cat and taking it under his arm, he hopes it does not have fleas! He gets back to the ground. The cat begins to purr. It is nice and warm in Sam's arms. Sliding on the mud, the dog runs up to sniff the cat. Sam shouts to the dog to stay away from the stray cat.

10b Reading Comprehension

Use the story to fill in the gaps:

Gus says they must rescue the _____ cat.
The dog jumps _____ and barks.
The cat _____ around the tree trunk.
Sam tells Gus not to make a _____.
Sam _____ onto the tree trunk.
Sam starts _____ his way up.
Sam hopes the cat does not have _____.
The cat begins to _____.
_____ on the mud, the dog runs up to sniff the cat.
Sam shouts to the dog to _____ away.

10c Picture

There are 4 words from the story in the picture below. Write the correct words underneath the box.

_____   _____   _____   _____

10d Crossword

Use the clues and the story to fill in the crossword:

Across
1. A kid shouts and screams but his mum says he is ____ a fuss. (6)
2. They bite and make you itch. (5)
3. The cat does this if it is happy. (4)

Down
1. Use it to smile. (5)
2. Slipping. (7)
3. Twists or ringlets. (5)
4. A lost pet (5)

10e Wordsorting

Below are 10 new words. Write them next to the correct letter group.

today   making   proud   each   burn
count   scream   nurse   railway   smoking

ou _____ _____   ing _____ _____

ea _____ _____   ay _____ _____

ur _____ _____

10f Choose your favourite part of the story. On a sheet of paper, draw a picture and write a sentence to describe it. Colour in your picture.

11. Vowel Blending and Endings
'aw', 'oi', 'all', 'er', 'ea'

Spelling Made Easy
Level 1 Textbook
Pages 36 - 42

11a Reading Exercise

It is dawn in the wood. It is Saturday. Sam has a wet cat under his arm. Sam's head is heavy with sleep. Sam and Gus have had no sleep for two days. They are ready for bed. Gus may fall over! Instead of bed, they are stuck in the wood at dawn, far from home. The soil is wet. It is awful! They have a dog and a cat but no bread. They start to walk. They reach a stone wall next to a big river. Gus starts talking as he is walking. The cat has sharp claws in its paws. Sam's arm hurts. The wood is full of noise from birds. Sam wants all the noise to stop. It seems to Sam that Gus is always talking. Sam thinks he may never, ever get home!

11b Reading Comprehension

Use the story to fill in the gaps:

It is _____ in the wood.
Sam's _____ is heavy with sleep.
The _____ is wet.
It is _____!
They have a _____ and a _____ but no _____.
They start to _____.
They reach a stone _____ next to a big _____.
The wood is full of _____ from birds.
Sam thinks he may never, _____ get home.

11c Picture

Use the story and the pictures to fill in the gaps.

Sam's _____ is _____ with sleep.

They reach a stone _____ next to a big _____.

The cat has sharp _____ in its _____.

The wood is full of _____ from birds.

11d Wordsearch

There 10 words from the story hidden in the box below. They go from left to right **AND** top to bottom.

m	j	a	p	m	u	f	a	l	l
z	s	l	d	a	v	b	j	m	x
s	c	l	m	w	j	e	f	l	h
d	f	i	s	f	m	v	u	k	e
p	a	w	h	u	k	e	b	j	a
c	m	x	s	l	t	r	y	h	v
z	h	b	r	e	a	d	j	k	y
r	i	v	e	r	t	y	m	x	n
c	f	m	z	c	d	s	o	i	l
l	k	n	o	i	s	e	u	j	m

11e Wordmuddle

Write the words below next to the correct letter group. Some of the words do not appear in the story.

    crawl   fall   driver   voice   over
    soil   breath   dawn   wall   head

all _____ _____   oi _____ _____

er _____ _____   ea _____ _____

aw _____ _____

11f On a sheet of paper, draw a picture of Sam and Gus with the dog and cat sitting on a stone wall next to a big river. Write a sentence underneath the picture to describe it.

12. Vowel Blending and Endings
   'aw', 'oi', 'all', 'er', 'ea'

Spelling Made Easy
Level 1 Textbook
Pages 36 - 42

14a Reading Exercise

Gus needs to go to the toilet and then go to bed. Dropping his jaw, he lets out a huge yawn. Gus makes a pile of straw and lies on it to go to sleep. Sam shouts that they must keep on walking. He makes a lot of noise. Gus has no choice but to get up and walk with Sam. Sam thinks he has never felt so dreadful. His breath smells. The dog seems fine. The cat has put away her claws and seems fine too. All the birds are singing in the trees. Sam and Gus are all sweaty. They reach a road and see a car. It swerves to avoid the kerb and stops. Sam can see the driver.

12b Reading Comprehension

Use the story to fill in the gaps:

Gus needs to go to the _____ and then go to bed.
Dropping his jaw, he lets out a huge _____.
Gus makes a pile of _____ and lies on it.
Sam thinks he has never felt so _____.
Sam shouts that they must keep on _____.
Gus has no _____ but to get up and walk.
Sam and Gus are all _____.
The car swerves to _____ the _____.
Sam can see the _____.

12c Pictures

Draw the correct picture in each box to match the word underneath.

jaw	toilet	driver

12d Crossword

Use the clues and the story to fill in the crossword:

Across
1. You feel really bad! (8)
2. A horse may sleep on this. (5)
3. Use your legs and feet to get from A to B. (4)

Down
1. Goes in and out to keep you alive! (6)
2. In charge of the car. (6)
3. Sharp bits at the end of a cat's paw. (5)
4. The loo. (6)
5. Make the car do this to avoid hitting a fox. (6)

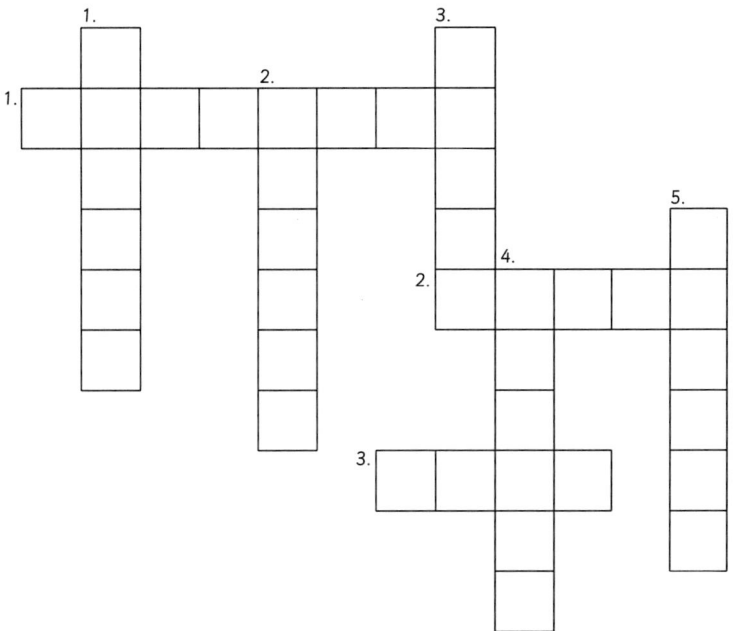

12e Wordsorting

Below are 10 new words. Write them next to the correct letter group.

| law | thunder | hall | spoil | number |
| small | voice | spread | saw | meant |

aw _____ _____   er _____ _____

oi _____ _____   ea _____ _____

all _____ _____

12f On a sheet of paper draw a picture of the car as it swerves to avoid the kerb. Write a sentence underneath the picture to describe it and colour it in.

13. Various
    'ow', 'igh', 'a', 'o', 'y'

Spelling Made Easy
Level 1 Textbook
Pages 44 – 52

13a Reading Exercise

Gus and Sam are waiting in the woods. A car pulls up. The driver of the car is Sue, Sam's wife. She has been out all night driving around, looking for Sam and Gus. She has a frown on her face. She had been thinking that Sam and Gus had drowned in the river. However, now she sees they are all right she is very cross. Sam and Sue have a row by the side of the road. Sue started driving around at midnight. She shouts at Sam and Gus. The cat is frightened and jumps from Sam's arms. Gus flops down on the grass, next to the path. He thinks he might pass out. He is afraid to ask for a lift into town. Gus has no money to spend. He has no mother, father or brother to look after him. He looks up at the sky. Sam and Gus think they might cry.

13b Reading Comprehension

Use the story to fill in the gaps:

Sue has been out all _____.
Sue has a _____ on her face.
Sam and Sue have a _____ by the side of the road.
Gus flops down on the _____.
Gus has no _____ to spend.
He thinks he might _____ out.
He has no _____, father or brother to look after him.
Gus looks up at the _____.
Sam and Gus think they might _____.

13c Pictures

Write the correct word from the story underneath each picture.

_____   _____   _____

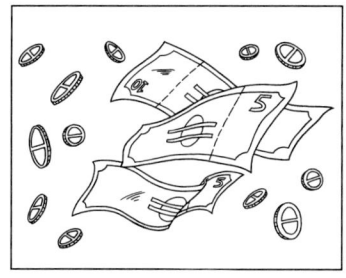   

_____   _____

13d Wordsearch

There are 10 words from the story hidden in the box below. They only go from left to right.

m	i	d	n	i	g	h	t	u	l
s	d	h	j	m	o	n	e	y	p
f	v	m	z	c	f	r	o	w	n
a	f	t	e	r	u	m	x	m	d
i	u	p	m	f	g	h	c	r	y
j	t	o	w	n	x	v	w	q	t
o	p	g	s	k	y	n	h	j	m
d	m	f	b	h	p	a	s	s	k
b	r	o	t	h	e	r	m	l	j
s	c	v	x	w	m	i	g	h	t

13e Wordmuddle

Write the words below next to the correct letter group. Some of the words do not appear in the story.

mother   town   cry   right   brow
might   path   front   class   shy

ow _____ _____   o _____ _____

igh _____ _____   y _____ _____

a _____ _____

13f On a separate sheet of paper, draw a picture of Sue starting her car on the garden path at midnight with a frown on her face. Colour in the picture and write a sentence underneath to describe it.

14. Various
  'ow', 'igh', 'a', 'o', 'y'

Spelling Made Easy
Level 1 Textbook
Pages 44 – 52

14a Reading Exercise

After two nights in the cold and wet, all Sam and Gus want to do is get home and dry. Sue gives Sam and Gus two gloves and a hat each. The dog and cat get in the car. Sue drives them all home rather fast. At home, Sue gives Sam and Gus a glass of milk and some food. There is a loaf of bread in the oven. Sam loves fresh bread. Sue says she will fry some bacon. There is a loud noise from the garden. Sam looks outside. There is a big crowd on the path. Sam asks Sue why they are there. Sue tells Sam that others in the town have been frightened for Sam and Gus. They have come to see they are safe. Sam is so happy he thinks he might cry but the crowd is so big he feels a bit shy.

14b Reading Comprehension

Use the story to fill in the gaps:

All Sam and Gus want to get to do is get home and _____.
Sue gives Sam and Gus two _____ each.
Sue drives them all home _____ fast.
Sue gives Sam and Gus a _____ of milk.
There is a loaf of bread in the _____.
Sue says she will _____ some bacon.
There is a big _____ on the path.
Sue tells Sam that others in the _____ have been _____ for Sam and Gus.
Sam is so happy he thinks he _____ cry.

14c Picture

There are 4 words from the story in the picture below. Write them underneath the box.

_____   _____   _____   _____

14d Crossword

Use the clues and the story to fill in the crossword:

Across
1. You may blush when you feel this. (3)
2. They keep your hands warm. (6)
3. You may do something. (5)
4. You do this if you are upset. (3)

Down
1. Will shatter if you drop it. (5)
2. Lots of people. (5)
3. You are afraid. (10)

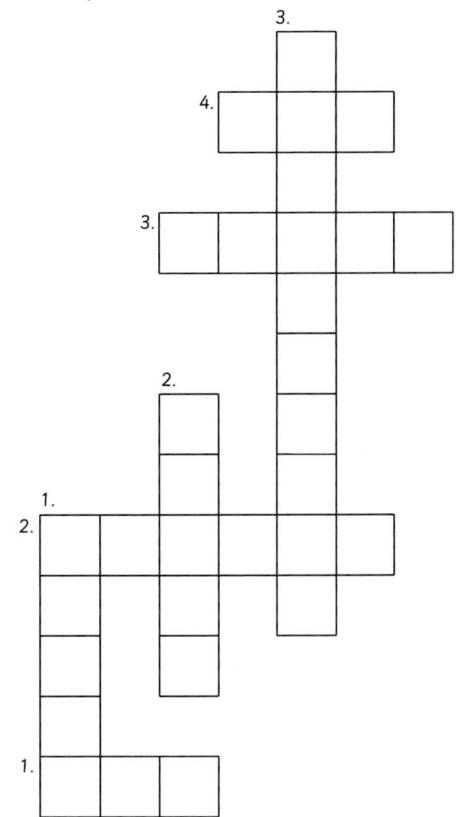

14e Wordsorting

Below are 10 new words. Write them next to the correct letter group.

last   how   spy   can't   month
high   trying   son   light   crown

ow _____ _____   o _____ _____

igh _____ _____   y _____ _____

a _____ _____

14f Choose your favourite sentence from the story. On a sheet of paper, draw a picture of it. Write a descriptive sentence underneath and colour in your picture.

15. Various
'ow', 'ew', 'tion', 'au', 'i', 'oy'

**Spelling Made Easy
Level 1 Textbook
Pages 54 – 62**

15a Reading Exercise

Sam looks out of the window. He can see the big crowd. They see him and point and shout. Sue lets them in. The first person is a small boy chewing gum. He asks Sam if he feels alright. Sam starts a conversation with the boy. He tells him he did not enjoy the trip but that he is feeling better now. All Sam's relations are in the room. There are quite a few! Sue finds a pint of fresh milk and makes them all a cup of tea, with a saucer. The house was tidy and now it is a mess but Sue does not mind. Sue is very kind. Sam has to tell his brother that the tent is ripped. He is a bit annoyed as it was new. They will have to go and find the tent tomorrow. Sam admits it was all his fault.

15b Reading Comprehension

Use the story to fill in the gaps:

Sam looks out of the _____.
The first person is a small _____ who is _____ gum.
Sam starts a _____ with the boy.
All Sam's _____ are in the room.
There are quite a _____!
Sue _____ a pint of fresh milk.
She makes them all a cup of tea with a _____.
The house was _____ and now it is a mess.
They will have to find the tent _____.
Sam's brother is _____ and Sam admits it was all his _____.

15c Pictures

Use the story and the pictures to fill in the gaps.

Sam has a _____
with a _____ chewing gum.

Sue finds a _____ of
fresh milk.

Sam's brother is _____ as the tent was _____.

Sam admits it was all his _____ and agrees to find the tent _____.

15d Wordsearch

There are 12 words from the story hidden in the box below. They go from left to right **AND** top to bottom.

z	r	y	n	e	w	v	x	s	g	u	w
p	y	v	n	d	x	s	g	m	r	h	i
m	f	a	u	l	t	a	y	t	e	x	n
g	k	l	i	m	v	b	q	w	l	m	d
t	o	m	o	r	r	o	w	x	a	z	o
d	f	g	b	v	d	l	t	y	t	n	w
p	o	f	g	k	i	n	d	h	i	j	l
i	m	e	z	j	m	g	f	e	o	r	y
n	b	w	h	j	u	y	m	s	n	e	m
t	o	p	m	s	a	u	c	e	r	a	p
f	y	a	n	n	o	y	e	d	m	h	q
c	o	n	v	e	r	s	a	t	i	o	n

15e Wordmuddle

Write the words below next to the correct letter group. Some of the words do not appear in the story.

fault   lion   snow   tidy   action   toy
window   relation   screw   annoy   autumn   new

ow _____ _____   au _____ _____

ew _____ _____   i _____ _____

tion _____ _____   oy _____ _____

15f On a sheet of paper draw a picture of Sue with a pint of milk making a cup of tea with a saucer for Sam's relations. Write a sentence to describe the picture and colour it in.

16. Various
   'ow', 'ew', 'tion', 'au', 'i', 'oy'

Spelling Made Easy
Level 1 Textbook
Pages 54 – 62

16a Reading Exercise

The crowd leaves Sam's house. Gus feels sad. He has had no relations since he was a boy. Sam finds Gus in the sitting room, looking out of the window. Gus blows his nose. Sam takes Gus's elbow and tells him he does not need relations. Sam wants to give Gus an invitation to become his brother. Gus throws his arms around Sam. He is so happy. Sam says Gus can use his automatic car if he likes. Sam goes to bed and is asleep as soon as his head hits the pillow. Gus goes to his new bedroom. It is so tidy! He is full of joy. He can see the station from the window. He pulls the blinds and lies down on the bed. He thinks he will enjoy being Sam's brother. For the first time he will have a home for the autumn. He blew his nose so hard it is now sore!

16b Reading Comprehension

Use the story to fill in the gaps:

Gus has had no relations since he was a _____.
Gus _____ his nose.
Sam wants to give Gus an _____ to become his brother.
Gus _____ his arms around Sam.
Sam says Gus can use his _____ car.
Gus's _____ bedroom is so _____!
Gus is full of _____.
He can see the _____ from the window.
He pulls the _____.
Gus will have a home for the _____.
He _____ his nose so hard it is now sore!

16c Pictures

Draw a picture of each word in the boxes provided. 3 words are new.

pillow	boy	station

16d Crossword

Use the clues and the story to fill in the crossword:

Across
1. Put your head on it to sleep. (6)
2. To fling or chuck. (5)
3. 'Come to my party!' (10)

Down
1. Gus did this to his nose (4)
2. A member of the family. (8)
3. Season when leaves fall. (6)
4. Pull down to keep the sun out. (5)
5. To have a good time. (5)

16e Wordsorting

Below are 12 new words. Write them next to the correct letter group.

| mind | action | toy | drew | mow | behind |
| enjoyed | follow | August | direction | haunted | grew |

ow _____ _____   au _____ _____

ew _____ _____   i _____ _____

tion _____ _____   oy _____ _____

16f Draw a picture of Gus in his new, tidy room. Label all his new things and then colour in your picture.

17. Various
   'ear', 'ai', 'ou', 'a', 'ph'

Spelling Made Easy
Level 1 Textbook
Pages 64 – 72

17a Reading Exercise

The next morning, Sue wakes Sam and Gus. It is nearly time to go and find the tent. Sam's brother Philip is on his way. Sam brushes his hair and goes downstairs. Gus is still in bed upstairs. Sam's younger brother pulls up outside in his car. Sam's brother knows the countryside very well. He thinks he knows where the tent is. When they find it, Philip will have to repair it. Sam hopes he is not in too much trouble. Sue goes to get Gus. Gus does not want to get up. Sue makes him wash his face and swallow a mug of tea. Sue tells Gus to brush his beard and hair. Sam, Gus and Philip leave to go to the wood. Sam says he will call Sue on his mobile phone when they get there.

17b Reading Comprehension

Use the story to fill in the gaps.

It is _____ time to find the tent.
Sam's brother _____ is on his way.
Gus is still in bed _____.
Sam's _____ brother pulls up outside.
Sam's brother knows the _____ very well.
When they find the tent, Philip will have to _____ it.
Sue makes Gus _____ his face and _____ a mug of tea.
Sue tells Gus to brush his _____ and hair.
Sam will call Sue on his mobile _____.

17c Pictures

Write the correct word from the story underneath each picture.

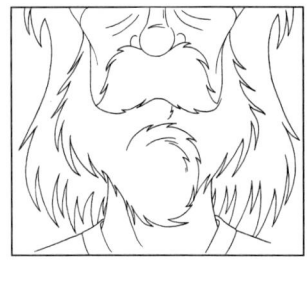  

_____   _____   _____

_____   _____

17d Wordsearch

*There are 10 words from the story hidden in the box below. They go from left to right **AND** top to bottom.*

u	p	s	t	a	i	r	s	m	g	i	b
m	t	y	h	c	m	s	g	g	p	a	e
u	x	w	p	l	g	d	x	a	h	z	a
b	n	a	r	e	p	a	i	r	o	y	r
t	y	s	m	z	c	b	f	a	n	h	d
i	b	h	g	j	k	f	m	d	e	m	o
a	q	m	x	c	y	o	u	n	g	e	r
s	w	a	l	l	o	w	h	k	c	e	g
y	u	i	v	m	s	v	x	s	m	o	l
n	e	a	r	l	y	m	f	h	b	s	z
w	q	s	f	p	h	i	l	i	p	j	b
o	m	i	t	r	o	u	b	l	e	a	m

17e Wordmuddle

Write the words below next to the correct heading. Some of the words do not appear in the story.

    beard   younger   wash   phone   swan
     pair   elephant   tears   hair   touch

ear _____ _____   ph _____ _____

ai _____ _____   a _____ _____

ou _____ _____

17f On a sheet of paper, draw a picture of Philip repairing his tent in the countryside. Write a sentence describing your picture it and then colour it in.

18. Various
   'ear', 'ai', 'ou', 'a', 'ph'

Spelling Made Easy
Level 1 Textbook
Pages 64 – 72

18a Reading Exercise

Sam shows Philip a couple of photos of the spot where they left the tent. Philip knows the place. He drives there fast. Sam sees the pond next to the wood where all the trouble began. It is deep in the countryside. No wonder Sam and Gus got so lost. Philip pulls over and they get out. The air is clear and bright. There is a pair of swans on the pond. There are ducks too. Philip sees his yellow tent in a tree. They pull it down. It is ripped right down the middle. Gus strokes his beard. Philip looks annoyed. Sam is nearly in tears. Philip has had the tent for less than a year and now it is past repair. It is all Sam's fault. He tries to phone Sue. A wasp is buzzing around. Philip swats it away.

18b Reading Comprehension

Use the story to fill in the gaps:

Sam shows Philip a _____ of _____ of the spot.
Sam sees the pond where all the _____ began.
The air is _____ and bright.
There is a _____ of _____ on the pond.
Sam is nearly in _____.
_____ looks annoyed.
The tent is now past _____.
Philip _____ the wasp away.

18c Picture

There are 4 words from the story in the picture below. Write the correct words in the spaces underneath the box.

_____   _____   _____   _____

18d Crossword

Use the clues and the story to fill in the crossword:

Across
1. A big, white bird. (4)
2. A pair. (6)
3. You get a telling off! (7)
4. To mend. (6)

Down
1. The air is _____ and bright. (5)
2. A real picture. (5)
3. Hair on a man's chin. (5)
4. Sam's brother. (6)

18e Wordsorting

Below are 10 new words. Write them next to the correct heading.

swap	touched	chair	clear	microphone
dear	fair	elephant	squash	double

ear _____ _____	ph _____ _____

ai _____ _____	a _____ _____

ou _____ _____

18f Choose your favourite part of the story. On a sheet of paper draw a picture of it and write a sentence to describe it. Colour it in.

19. Various
    'o', 'are', 'ough', 'ar'

Spelling Made Easy
Level 1 Textbook
Pages 74 - 80

19a Reading Exercise

Both Sam and Gus feel very sorry about the tent. All three men stand and stare at the ripped tent. It had been a gift from Philip and Sam's parents. They bought it for Philip to use with his wife when it was nice and warm. It was a reward for some hard work Philip had done in their garden. A hare runs past. It stops to have a look at the tent. Sam coughs and the scared hare runs away. Philip drops the tent in a bin. It is of no use to him now. It is totally broken. Philip says his wife must also be told. Sam is scared of Philip's wife. If Sam had only found out how to put up the tent he may not have broken it!

19b Reading Comprehension

Use the story to fill in the gaps:

_____ Sam and Gus feel sorry about the tent.
They stand and _____ at the ripped tent.
Philip's parents _____ it for him.
It was a _____ for some hard work.
It was for Philip and his wife to use when it was nice and _____.
A _____ runs past.
Sam _____ and the scared hare runs away.
If Sam had found out how to put the tent up, he might not have _____ it.

19c Pictures

Write the correct word from the story underneath the picture.

_____   _____

   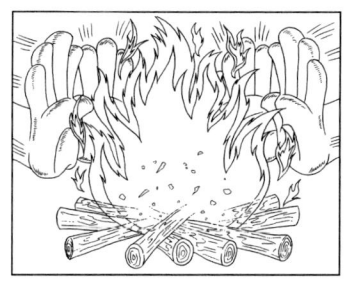

_____   _____

19d Wordsearch

There are 8 words from the story hidden in the box below. They go from left to right **AND** top to bottom.

s	c	o	u	g	h	a	b	u	k
x	b	j	m	d	f	h	o	v	m
b	r	o	k	e	n	m	u	e	r
m	e	s	d	f	c	x	g	z	e
o	h	w	a	r	m	j	h	k	w
n	t	m	u	i	p	b	t	g	a
l	f	g	v	s	t	z	j	m	r
y	m	p	a	r	e	n	t	s	d
q	e	d	z	m	u	a	p	b	f
o	s	c	a	r	e	d	m	f	g

19e Wordmuddle

Write the words below next to the correct letter group. Some of the words do not appear in the story.

    only   hare   reward   sold
  warning   rough   care   bought

o _____ _____   ough _____ _____

are _____ _____   ar _____ _____

19f On a sheet of paper draw a picture of Sam coughing at the hare in the wood. Write a sentence underneath to describe your picture and colour it in.

20. Various
  '0', 'are', 'ough', 'ar'

Spelling Made Easy
Level 1 Textbook
Pages 74 - 80

20a Reading Exercise

Sam tells Philip that he has enough money to get a new tent. They stop at a shop on the way back. Sam buys a new gold tent. It is very big. The old tent was only a quarter of the size of the new tent. The shopkeeper is very happy to have sold the gold tent. It costs Sam a lot of money, but he does not mind. Sam always does what he ought to, however painful or costly it is! Philip says that they can all share the new tent. He says they can go camping with their parents when it is warm enough. Sam tells Philip he does not dare. He and Gus have had enough camping to last a lifetime!

20b Reading Comprehension

Use the story to fill in the gaps:

Sam has _____ money to get a new tent.
Sam buys a new _____ tent.
The old tent was only a _____ of the size of the new tent.
The shopkeeper is happy to have _____ the gold tent.
Sam always does what he _____ to.
Philip says they can _____ the new tent.
They can go camping with their parents when it is _____ enough.
Sam tells Philip he does not _____.

20c Pictures

Draw a picture of each new word in the boxes provided.

postman

hare

20d Crossword

Use the clues and the story to fill in the crossword

Across
1. Not too hot. (4)
2. To split with a friend. (5)
3. No more please! (6)
4. A metal for making wedding rings. (4)

Down
1. Your Mum and Dad. (7)
2. Half of a half. (7)
3. Not young. (3)
4. A moral feeling. (5)

20e Wordsorting

Below are 8 new words. Write them next to the correct letter group.

most   spare   tough   told
rough   warn   fare   ward

o _____ _____   ough _____ _____

are _____ _____   ar _____ _____

20f Draw a picture of Sam, Philip and their parents with their gold tent on a warm day. Write a descriptive sentence underneath and colour in your picture.

ANSWERS (pages 2-3)

1. Short Vowel Sounds
'a', 'o', 'e', 'i', 'u'

Spelling Made Easy
Level 1 Textbook
Pages 10 – 14

1b Reading Comprehension

Use the story to help fill in the gaps:

Sam has a **pal**.
Sam will camp in a **tent**.
Sam and the tramp will camp next to a **pond**.
Sam has a picnic in a **string** bag.
The tramp will bang his **drum**.
Sam's **dog** will go with the men.
The dog can **smell** the crisps in the bag.
Sam **scrubs** his hands.
The tramp rips the **bag** of crisps.
He lets the dog have a **sniff**.

1c Write the correct word underneath each picture.

| **tent** | **pond** | **bag** |
| **drum** | **string** | |

1d Wordsearch

t	r	a	m	p	q	w	t	m	o
a	p	o	n	d	m	j	l	k	p
v	f	g	y	u	s	n	i	f	f
s	m	e	l	e	z	u	i	p	
z	x	f	d	r	u	m	t	y	n
s	t	r	o	n	g	r	g	b	m
q	t	m	a	b	a	n	g	c	k
n	o	y	h	m	n	e	x	t	l
s	c	r	u	b	d	w	m	e	r
m	f	p	i	c	n	i	c	h	j

1e Wordmuddle

a	**hand**	**bank**	o	**cost**	**dog**
e	**desk**	**smell**	u	**scrub**	**plug**
i	**drink**	**king**			

ANSWERS (pages 4-5)

2. Short Vowel Sounds
'a', 'o', 'e', 'i', 'u'

Spelling Made Easy
Level 1 Textbook
Pages 10 – 14

2b Use the story to help fill in the gaps:

Sam and the **tramp** are on a trip.
Sam **must** put up the tent.
Sam has one **canvas**.
Sam has a **hundred** pegs.
Sam will have his **mint** drink.
He sits **next** to the tramp.
Sam and the tramp have their picnic next to the **pond**.
The dog gets the **rest** of the crisps.
A **frog** jumps up from the pond.
The frog **sits** on the drum.

2c Picture

dog   **frog**   **bag**   **crisps**   **pegs**

2d Crossword

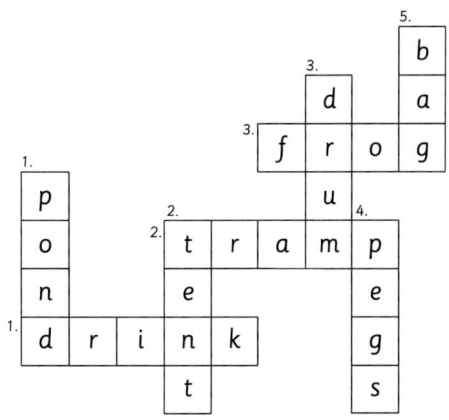

2e Wordsorting

a	**scrap**	**sprang**	o	**drop**	**frost**
e	**left**	**yell**	u	**lump**	**bunk**
i	**ring**	**sting**			

ANSWERS (pages 6-7)

3. Vowel Blending and Consonant Clusters
'ck', 'ee', 'oo', 'ar', 'or'

Spelling Made Easy
Level 1 Textbook
Pages 15 - 19

3b Reading Comprehension

Use the story to help fill in the gaps:

Sam must be **quick** as it is dark.
Sam, the tramp and the dog will **sleep** in the tent.
The **wood** is next to the pond.
A frog jumps onto Sam's **arm**.
A **duck** steps up from the pond.
It starts to peck Sam's **heel**.
Sam can see **forty** ducks on the pond.
The tramp sits on a **stool**.
The dog starts to **bark**.
Soon it will be **morning**.

3c Pictures

A frog jumps onto Sam's **arm**.

A **bee** stings Sam's leg.

The **duck** pecks Sam's **heel**.

The **wood** is next to the pond.

3c Wordsearch

q	u	i	c	k	m	p	z	a	r
d	f	g	m	y	s	t	a	r	t
t	n	s	o	o	n	k	l	u	f
c	b	a	r	k	v	m	b	k	d
x	v	b	f	o	r	t	y	m	l
b	w	f	t	m	s	l	e	e	p
a	m	o	r	n	i	n	g	i	o
f	v	w	o	o	d	u	m	j	k
s	e	e	f	y	t	r	s	x	m
m	o	k	l	g	d	d	u	c	k

3d Wordmuddle

ck	**peck**	clock	or	**forty**	born
ee	**heel**	need	ar	**bark**	car
oo	**pool**	wood			

ANSWERS (pages 8-9)

4. Vowel Blending and Consonant Clusters
'ck', 'ee', 'oo', 'ar', 'or'

Spelling Made Easy
Level 1 Textbook
Pages 15 – 19

4b Reading Comprehension

Use the story to fill in the gaps:

Sam **needs** help!
The frog is on Sam's **arm**.
Sam's leg starts to **smart**.
The tramp bangs his **boots** hard.
The duck runs **back** into the pond.
Sam sees that the canvas is **torn**.
It is not a **good** start to the trip!
Sam and the tramp have a quick **snack**.
They must not be **greedy**.
They must not be greedy **for** they need to mend the tent.

4d Crossword

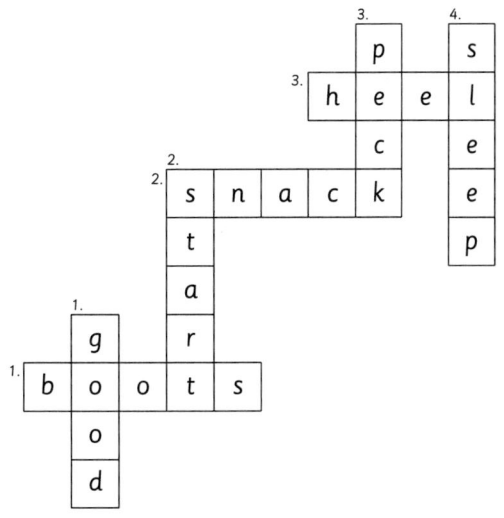

4e Wordsorting

ck	**luck**	**trick**	oo	**look**	**broom**
ee	**seed**	**queen**	or	**more**	**story**
ar	**farm**	**garden**			

ANSWERS (pages 10-11)

5. Consonant Clusters and Magic 'e'
'sh', 'ch', 'th', 'a-e', 'i-e'

Spelling Made Easy
Level 1 Textbook
Pages 20 - 24

5b Reading Comprehension

Use the story to help fill in the gaps:

The tramp's **name** is Gus.
Gus **blames** Sam for the fact that he has had no sleep.
Sam and Gus have **lunch**.
Sam has **chicken** and chips.
Sam **likes** the taste of chicken.
A **thrush** starts to sing.
They rush into the pond and make a big **splash**.
It is **nice** and cool in the pond.
Sam makes a **ship** from twigs and a sheet of **cloth**.

5c Pictures

    bench   **fish**   **thrush**

        face   **pie**

5d Wordsearch

t	h	e	y	t	r	m	n	l	n
m	s	h	e	e	t	j	t	i	a
f	g	h	j	v	m	a	l	l	m
b	e	n	c	h	u	y	s	v	e
z	s	m	i	l	e	y	t	r	b
x	q	f	b	n	c	g	e	p	v
n	i	c	e	g	l	p	j	m	s
b	m	o	k	l	o	d	s	c	h
j	k	p	t	m	t	e	f	x	i
c	h	i	p	s	h	d	m	b	p

5e Wordmuddle

sh	**ship**	**rush**	a-e	**taste**	**came**
ch	**chips**	**such**	i-e	**ride**	**smile**
th	**cloth**	**thud**			

ANSWERS (pages 12-13)

6. Consonant Clusters and Magic 'e'
'sh', 'ch', 'th', 'a-e', 'i-e'

Spelling Made Easy
Level 1 Textbook
Pages 20 - 24

6b Reading Comprehension

Use the story to help fill in the gaps:

The dog jumps onto Sam's **chest** with a big **crash**.
It makes such a **splash** and lots of **froth**.
Gus **slides** on the mud in the pond.
Gus hits his **cheek** on the dog's leg.
Sam rubs the dog with a **cloth**.
The dog **shakes**.
Sam and Gus **lie** in the hot sun.
When they **wake** it is dark.
They still have no tent.

6c Picture

cloth   **cheek**   **chest**   **five**

6d Crossword

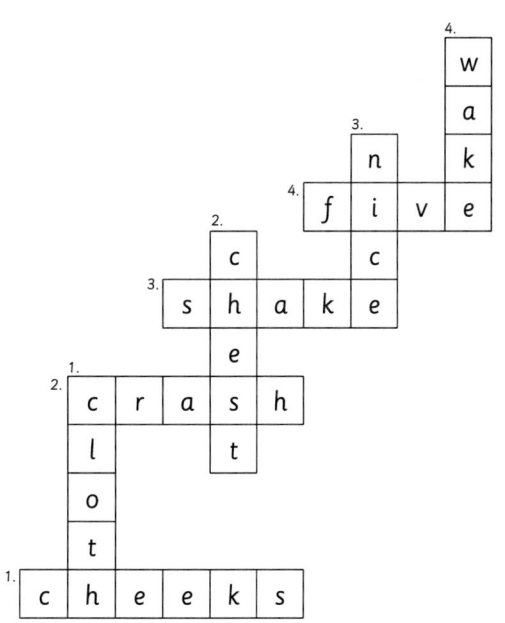

6e Wordsorting

sh	**shot**	**cash**	a-e	**came**	**wave**
ch	**chop**	**crunch**	i-e	**drive**	**tie**
th	**thing**	**moth**			

ANSWERS (pages 14-15)

7. Vowel Blending and Magic 'e'
'o-e', u-e', 'ai', 'oa', 'ir'

Spelling Made Easy
Level 1 Textbook
Pages 25 - 29

7b Reading Comprehension

Use the story to help fill in the gaps:

Sam and Gus are **alone** in the dark wood.
They are far from **home**.
It starts to **rain**.
Sam and Gus have no **coats**.
They run to a big **fir** tree.
The rain has made them wet **again**.
It is not good to have rain in **June**.
Sam hates **toads** and snails.
Gus had no **clue** that Sam is afraid of toads.
The dog is **thirsty**.

7c Pictures

Sam and Gus are far from **home** and have no **coats**.

Sam and Gus run to a big **fir** tree to hide from the **rain**.

Sam hates **snails** and **toads**.

Gus had no **clue** that Sam hates toads.

7d Wordsearch

d	i	r	t	y	r	y	n	f	k
s	d	b	p	h	o	n	e	a	e
f	m	c	u	m	o	a	n	i	m
v	a	o	f	e	x	t	z	n	t
j	x	a	g	s	h	j	m	t	h
u	c	t	m	i	m	y	g	k	i
n	v	s	a	g	a	i	n	m	r
e	b	m	z	t	g	n	d	a	s
m	j	b	l	u	e	u	l	j	t
g	a	l	o	n	e	m	f	p	y

7e Wordmuddle

o-e	**home**	**rose**	ir	**girl**	**thirsty**
u-e	**blue**	**clue**	ai	**nail**	**afraid**
oa	**coat**	**roast**			

ANSWERS (pages 16-17)

8. Vowel Blending and Magic 'e'
'o-e', u-e', 'ai', 'oa', 'ir'

**Spelling Made Easy
Level 1 Textbook
Pages 25 – 29**

8b Reading Comprehension

Use the story to fill in the gaps:

Gus gets his **flute** and makes a tune.
Gus smiles, but Sam **groans**.
Sam is thirsty and **dirty**.
Sam has a **pain** in his nose.
Sam's wish is to be in his bed at **home**.
There are **loads** of toads.
They look like **stones**.
They have no **clue** where they can be.
There are **thirty** tracks into the woods.
They are lost and Gus is **afraid**.

8d Crossword

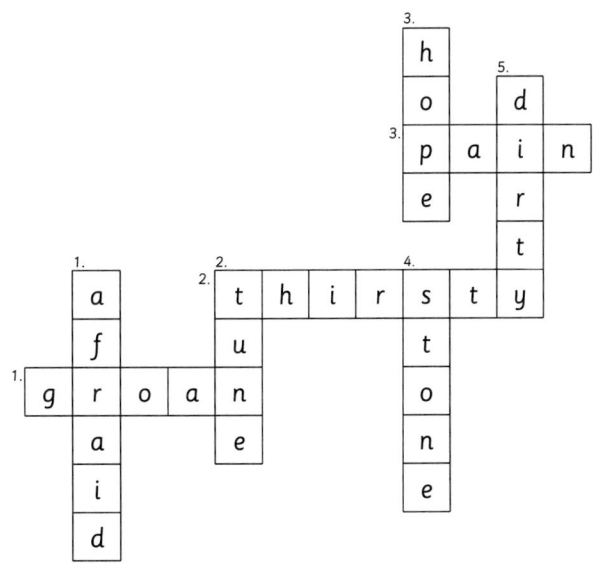

8e Wordsorting

ai	**paint**	**sail**	o-e	**close**	**note**
oa	**soak**	**coal**	u-e	**true**	**glue**
ir	**girl**	**stir**			

49

ANSWERS (pages 18-19)

9. Vowel Blending and Endings
'ou', 'ea', 'ay', ing', 'ur'

Spelling Made Easy
Level 1 Textbook
Pages 30 - 35

9b Reading Comprehension

Use the story to help fill in the gaps:

Sam tells Gus that the next **day** will be Saturday.
Gus smiles and says they **may** be under the tree until next Wednesday.
Hoping that Gus is just **joking** Sam shouts for help.
The dog runs up at the **sound** of Sam shouting.
The dog's **fur** is wet from the rain.
Sam wants to get back to his **house**.
The dog digs up a **turnip**.
Sam is dreaming of **peach** ice-cream.
Gus just wants a cup of **tea**.

9c Pictures

turnip   **peach**   **shouting**

   hay   **house**

9d Wordsearch

m	s	f	h	j	y	u	m	a	y
c	r	e	a	m	r	t	v	d	a
g	h	k	l	t	a	k	i	n	g
z	v	t	m	s	o	u	n	d	m
j	o	k	i	n	g	x	c	h	f
w	m	o	h	a	y	p	f	d	r
t	h	u	r	s	d	a	y	m	t
y	s	h	o	u	t	u	e	c	v
x	c	m	d	f	g	h	t	e	a
f	u	r	z	y	x	m	g	j	u

9e Wordmuddle

ou	**house**	**mouth**	ay	**tray**	**may**
ea	**tea**	**please**	ur	**fur**	**church**
ing	**sliding**	**hoping**			

ANSWERS (pages 20-21)

10. Vowel Blending and Endings
'ou', 'ea', 'ay', ing', 'ur'

Spelling Made Easy
Level 1 Textbook
Pages 30 - 35

10b Reading Comprehension

Use the story to fill in the gaps:

Gus says they must rescue the **stray** cat.
The dog jumps **about** and barks.
The cat **curls** around the tree trunk.
Sam tells Gus not to make a **sound**.
Sam **leaps** onto the tree trunk.
Sam starts **making** his way up.
Sam hopes the cat does not have **fleas**.
The cat begins to **purr**.
Sliding on the mud, the dog runs up to sniff the cat.
Sam shouts to the dog to **stay** away.

10c Picture

flea   **tree**   **sliding**   **ground**

10d Crossword

				4.
		3.		s
		c		t
3. p	u	r	r	
		r		a
2.	s	l		y
2. f	l	e	a	s
	i			
	d			
1. m	a	k	i	n	g
	o		n	
	u		g	
	t			
	h			

10e Wordsorting

ou	**proud**	**count**	ing	**smoking**	**making**
ea	**each**	**scream**	ay	**today**	**railway**
ur	**nurse**	**burn**			

ANSWERS (pages 22-23)

11. Vowel Blending and Endings
'aw', 'oi', 'all', 'er', 'ea'

Spelling Made Easy
Level 1 Textbook
Pages 36 - 42

11b Reading Comprehension

Use the story to fill in the gaps:

It is **dawn** in the wood.
Sam's **head** is heavy with sleep.
The **soil** is wet.
It is **awful**!
They have a **dog** and a **cat** but no **bread**.
They start to **walk**.
They reach a stone **wall** next to a big **river**.
The wood is full of **noise** from birds.
Sam thinks he may never, **ever** get home.

11c Pictures

Sam's **head** is
heavy with sleep.

They reach a stone **wall**
next to a big **river**.

The cat has sharp **claws**
in its **paws**.

The wood is full of **noise**
from birds.

11d Wordsearch

m	j	*a*	p	m	u	*f*	*a*	*l*	*l*
z	s	*l*	d	*a*	v	b	j	m	x
s	c	*l*	m	*w*	j	*e*	*f*	*l*	*h*
d	*f*	i	s	*f*	m	v	u	k	*e*
p	*a*	*w*	h	u	k	*e*	b	j	*a*
c	m	x	s	*l*	t	*r*	y	h	*v*
z	h	*b*	*r*	*e*	*a*	*d*	j	k	*y*
r	*i*	*v*	*e*	*r*	t	y	m	x	n
c	*f*	m	z	c	d	*s*	*o*	*i*	*l*
l	k	*n*	*o*	*i*	*s*	*e*	u	j	m

11e Wordmuddle

all	**fall**	**wall**		oi	**voice**	**soil**
er	**driver**	**over**		ea	**breath**	**head**
aw	**crawl**	**dawn**				

ANSWERS (pages 24-25)

12. Vowel Blending and Endings
'aw', 'oi', 'all', 'er', 'ea'

Spelling Made Easy
Level 1 Textbook
Pages 36 - 42

12b Reading Comprehension

Use the story to fill in the gaps:

Gus needs to go to the **toilet** and then go to bed.
Dropping his jaw, he lets out a huge **yawn**.
Gus makes a pile of **straw** and lies on it.
Sam thinks he has never felt so **dreadful**.
Sam shouts that they must keep on **walking**.
Gus has no **choice** but to get up and walk.
Sam and Gus are all **sweaty**.
The car swerves to **avoid** the **kerb**.
Sam can see the **driver**.

12d Crossword

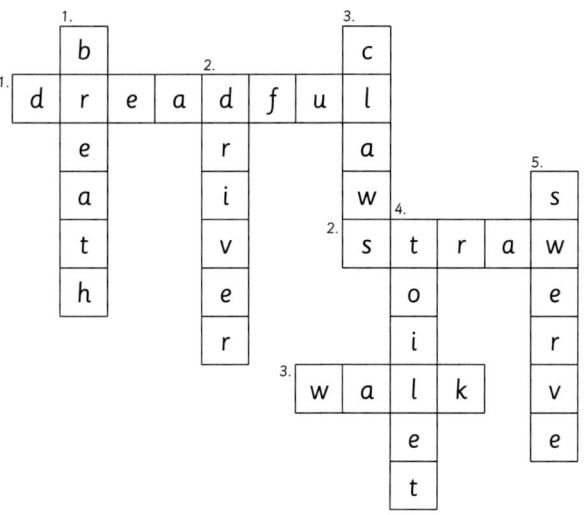

12e Wordsorting

aw	**law**	**saw**	er	**thunder**	**number**
oi	**spoil**	**voice**	ea	**meant**	**spread**
all	**small**	**hall**			

ANSWERS (pages 26-27)

13. Various
'ow', 'igh', 'a', 'o', 'y'

**Spelling Made Easy
Level 1 Textbook
Pages 44 – 52**

13b Reading Comprehension

Use the story to fill in the gaps:

Sue has been out all **night**.
Sue has a **frown** on her face.
Sam and Sue have a **row** by the side of the road.
Gus flops down on the **grass**.
Gus has no **money** to spend.
He thinks he might **pass** out.
He has no **mother**, father or brother to look after him.
Gus looks up at the **sky**.
Sam and Gus think they might **cry**.

13c Pictures

cry   **night**   **frown**

money   **drown**

13d Wordsearch

m	i	d	n	i	g	h	t	u	l
s	d	h	j	m	o	n	e	y	p
f	v	m	z	c	f	r	o	w	n
a	f	t	e	r	u	m	x	m	d
i	u	p	m	f	g	h	c	r	y
j	t	o	w	n	x	v	w	q	t
o	p	g	s	k	y	n	h	j	m
d	m	f	b	h	p	a	s	s	k
b	r	o	t	h	e	r	m	l	j
s	c	v	x	w	m	i	g	h	t

13e Wordmuddle

ow	**town**	**brow**	o	**mother**	**front**
igh	**might**	**right**	y	**shy**	**cry**
a	**path**	**class**			

ANSWERS (pages 28-29)

14. Various
'ow', 'igh', 'a', 'o', 'y'

Spelling Made Easy
Level 1 Textbook
Pages 44 – 52

14b Reading Comprehension

Use the story to fill in the gaps:

All Sam and Gus want to get to do is get home and **dry**.
Sue gives Sam and Gus two **gloves** each.
Sue drives them all home **rather** fast.
Sue gives Sam and Gus a **glass** of milk.
There is a loaf of bread in the **oven**.
Sue says she will **fry** some bacon.
There is a big **crowd** on the path.
Sue tells Sam that others in the **town** have been **frightened** for Sam and Gus.
Sam is so happy he thinks he **might** cry.

14c Picture

glass **bacon** **crowd** **oven**

14d Crossword

Across: 4. cry, 3. might, 2. gloves, 1. shy
Down: 3. frightened, 2. crowd, 1. glass

14e Wordsorting

ow	crown	how	o	son	month
igh	high	light	y	trying	spy
a	can't	last			

ANSWERS (pages 30-31)

15. Various
'ow', 'ew', 'tion', 'au', 'i', 'oy'

Spelling Made Easy
Level 1 Textbook
Pages 54 – 62

15b Reading Comprehension

Use the story to fill in the gaps:

Sam looks out of the **window**.
The first person is a small **boy** who is **chewing** gum.
Sam starts a **conversation** with the boy.
All Sam's **relations** are in the room.
There are quite a **few**!
Sue **finds** a pint of fresh milk.
She makes them all a cup of tea with a **saucer**.
The house was **tidy** and now it is a mess.
They will have to find the tent **tomorrow**.
Sam's brother is **annoyed** and Sam admits it was all his **fault**.

15c Pictures

Sam has a **conversation** with a **boy** chewing gum.

Sue finds a **pint** of fresh milk.

Sam's brother is **annoyed** as the tent was **new**.

Sam admits it was all his **fault** and agrees to find the tent **tomorrow**.

15d Wordsearch

z	r	y	**n**	**e**	**w**	v	x	s	g	u	**w**
p	y	v	n	d	x	s	g	m	r	h	**i**
m	**f**	**a**	**u**	**l**	**t**	a	y	t	**e**	x	**n**
g	k	l	i	m	v	b	q	w	**l**	m	**d**
t	**o**	**m**	**o**	**r**	**r**	**o**	**w**	x	a	z	**o**
d	f	g	b	v	d	l	t	y	t	n	**w**
p	o	**f**	g	**k**	**i**	**n**	**d**	h	**i**	j	l
i	m	**e**	z	j	m	g	f	**e**	**o**	r	y
n	**b**	**w**	h	j	u	y	m	s	**n**	e	m
t	**o**	p	m	**s**	**a**	**u**	**c**	**e**	**r**	a	p
f	**y**	**a**	**n**	**n**	**o**	**y**	**e**	**d**	m	h	q
c	**o**	**n**	**v**	**e**	**r**	**s**	**a**	**t**	**i**	**o**	**n**

15e Wordmuddle

ow	**window**	**snow**	au	**autumn**	**fault**
ew	**screw**	**new**	i	**tidy**	**lion**
tion	**relation**	**action**	oy	**annoy**	**toy**

ANSWERS (pages 32-33)

16. Various
'ow', 'ew', 'tion', 'au', 'i', 'oy'

Spelling Made Easy
Level 1 Textbook
Pages 54 – 62

16b Reading Comprehension

Use the story to fill in the gaps:

Gus has had no relations since he was a **boy**.
Gus **blows** his nose.
Sam wants to give Gus an **invitation** to become his brother.
Gus **throws** his arms around Sam.
Sam says Gus can use his **automatic** car.
Gus's **new** bedroom is so **tidy**!
Gus is full of **joy**.
He can see the **station** from the window.
He pulls the **blinds**.
Gus will have a home for the **autumn**.
He **blew** his nose so hard it is now sore!

16d Crossword

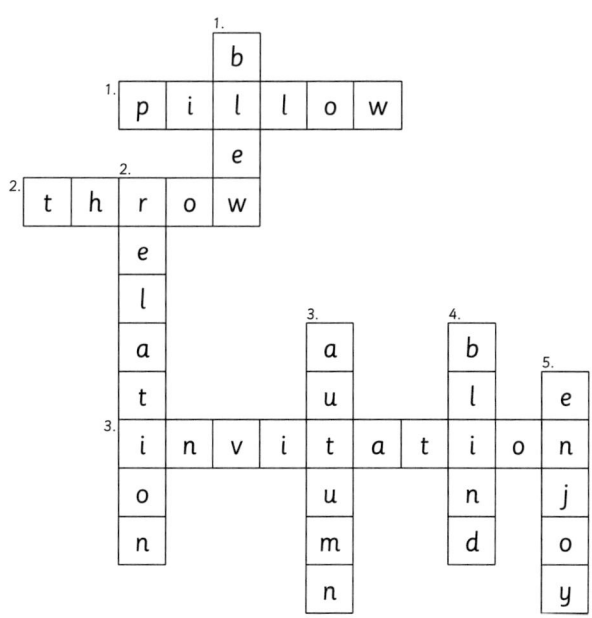

16e Wordsorting

ow	**follow**	**mow**	au	**August**	**haunted**
ew	**drew**	**grew**	i	**behind**	**mind**
tion	**action**	**direction**	oy	**toy**	**enjoyed**

ANSWERS (pages 34-35)

17. Various
    'ear', 'ai', 'ou', 'a', 'ph'

Spelling Made Easy
Level 1 Textbook
Pages 64 – 72

17b Reading Comprehension

Use the story to fill in the gaps.

It is **nearly** time to find the tent.
Sam's brother **Philip** is on his way.
Gus is still in bed **upstairs**.
Sam's **younger** brother pulls up outside.
Sam's brother knows the **countryside** very well.
When they find the tent, Philip will have to **repair** it.
Sue makes Gus **wash** his face and **swallow** a mug of tea.
Sue tells Gus to brush his **beard** and hair.
Sam will call Sue on his mobile **phone**.

17c Pictures

beard **hair** **wash**

countryside **phone**

17d Wordsearch

u	p	s	t	a	i	r	s	m	g	i	b
m	t	y	h	c	m	s	g	g	**p**	a	**e**
u	x	**w**	p	l	g	d	x	a	**h**	z	**a**
b	n	**a**	**r**	**e**	**p**	**a**	**i**	**r**	o	y	**r**
t	y	**s**	m	z	c	b	f	a	**n**	h	**d**
i	b	**h**	g	j	k	f	m	d	e	m	o
a	q	m	x	c	**y**	**o**	**u**	**n**	**g**	**e**	**r**
s	**w**	**a**	**l**	**l**	**o**	**w**	h	k	c	e	g
y	u	i	v	m	s	v	x	s	m	o	l
n	**e**	**a**	**r**	**l**	**y**	m	f	h	b	s	z
w	q	s	f	**p**	**h**	**i**	**l**	**i**	**p**	j	b
o	m	i	**t**	**r**	**o**	**u**	**b**	**l**	**e**	a	m

17e Wordmuddle

ear	**beard**	tears	ph	**phone**	elephant
ai	**pair**	hair	a	**swan**	wash
ou	**younger**	touch			

ANSWERS (pages 36-37)

18. Various
'ear', 'ai', 'ou', 'a', 'ph'

Spelling Made Easy
Level 1 Textbook
Pages 64 – 72

18b Reading Comprehension

Use the story to fill in the gaps:

Sam shows Philip a **couple** of **photos** of the spot.
Sam sees the pond where all the **trouble** began.
The air is **clear** and bright.
There is a **pair** of **swans** on the pond.
Sam is nearly in **tears**.
Philip looks annoyed.
The tent is now past **repair**.
Philip **swats** the wasp away.

18c Picture

photos   **beard**   **wasp**   **swan**

18d Crossword

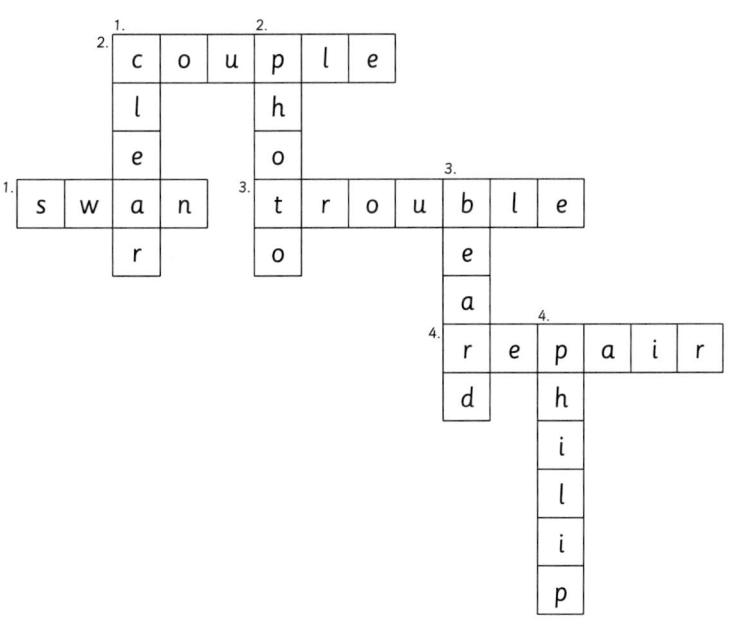

18e Wordsorting

ear	**clear**	**dear**	ph	**elephant**	**microphone**
ai	**fair**	**chair**	a	**swap**	**squash**
ou	**touched**	**double**			

ANSWERS (pages 38-39)

19. Various
    'o', 'are', 'ough', 'ar'

Spelling Made Easy
Level 1 Textbook
Pages 74 - 80

19b Reading Comprehension

Use the story to fill in the gaps:

Both Sam and Gus feel sorry about the tent.
They stand and **stare** at the ripped tent.
Philip's parents **bought** it for him.
It was a **reward** for some hard work.
It was for Philip and his wife to use when it was nice and **warm**.
A **hare** runs past.
Sam **coughs** and the scared hare runs away.
If Sam had found out how to put the tent up, he might not have **broken** it.

19c Pictures

        hare   **cough**

    broken   **warm**

19d Wordsearch

s	**c**	**o**	**u**	**g**	**h**	a	**b**	u	k
x	b	j	m	d	f	h	**o**	v	m
b	**r**	**o**	**k**	**e**	**n**	m	u	e	**r**
m	e	s	d	f	c	x	**g**	z	**e**
o	h	**w**	**a**	**r**	**m**	j	**h**	k	**w**
n	t	m	u	i	p	b	**t**	g	**a**
l	f	g	v	s	t	z	j	m	**r**
y	m	**p**	**a**	**r**	**e**	**n**	**t**	**s**	**d**
q	e	d	z	m	u	a	p	b	f
o	**s**	**c**	**a**	**r**	**e**	**d**	m	f	g

19e Wordmuddle

o	**only**	**sold**	ough	**rough**	**bought**
are	**care**	**hare**	ar	**reward**	**warning**

ANSWERS (pages 40-41)

20. Various
  'o', 'are', 'ough', 'ar'

**Spelling Made Easy
Level 1 Textbook
Pages 74 - 80**

20b Reading Comprehension

Use the story to fill in the gaps:

Sam has **enough** money to get a new tent.
Sam buys a new **gold** tent.
The old tent was only a **quarter** of the size of the new tent.
The shopkeeper is happy to have **sold** the gold tent.
Sam always does what he **ought** to.
Philip says they can **share** the new tent.
They can go camping with their parents when it is **warm** enough.
Sam tells Philip he does not **dare**.

20d Crossword

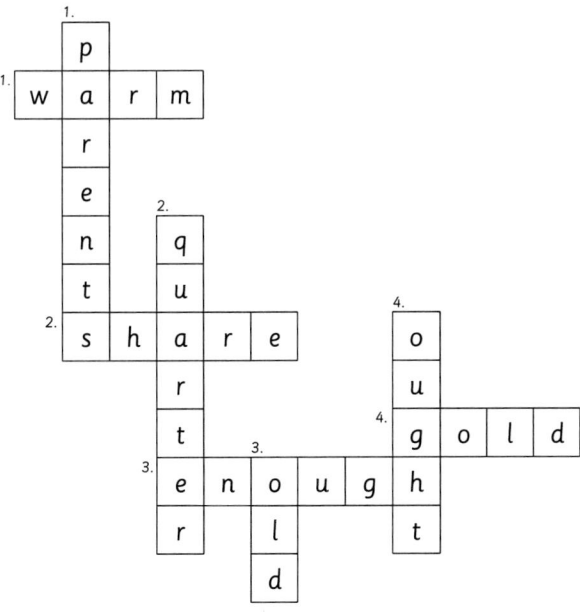

20e Wordsorting

| o | **most** | **told** | ough | **rough** | **tough** |
| are | *fare* | *spare* | ar | **warn** | **ward** |

DIGS AND BANGS
by Violet Brand

It was morning in the village of Brand's Patch. The sun shone in through the bedroom windows of a small house with a bright yellow door. Sam opened his eyes, gave a big yawn and rolled over to go back to sleep.

Then suddenly he remembered. Today was the big day! Brand's Patch band would march through the park at 3 o'clock this afternoon. The whole village would come out to watch.

Sam was wide-awake now! He jumped out of bed and rushed downstairs.

Sam's wife Sue always gets up earlier than Sam. Sue is always nicely dressed. She was already cleaning the kitchen floor when Sam rushed in.

"Good morning!" said Sam cheerily.

"Well just look at your shirt and trousers. You look awful!" Sue said snappily.

"Today is the day you will march through the village," Sue carried on, "and your clothes are a mess."

Sam's face fell as he looked down at himself. Sue was right. He couldn't go out like that.

"Take off your shirt" said Sue, picking up the iron, "and do up your trousers!"

Sam took off his shirt and did up his trousers. His tummy stuck out and he could not see his feet. Trust Sue to make him feel sad! But then he remembered how much fun last year's march had been.

Sam had played the triangle very well and very loud. Bernard the Bandmaster had even told him that he might be allowed to bang the big drum this year! Gosh! Think how many people would look at him then!

Sam was smiling again now. He took his clean shirt from Sue and said, "Last year I played the triangle but this year I hope to play the drum! I am very excited."

"Don't be so silly," said Sue. "Of course you won't play the drum. Jim is home from his holiday and he always plays the drum. Jim always wears smart clothes and has polished shoes. He deserves to play the drum."

Sam sighed. His smile was gone again.

"Jim can carry the drum in his big, red car," Sue went on. "How could you carry it on your bent, blue bike? No Sam, you must play the triangle because you are scruffy and you have no big, red car. Only a bent, blue bike."

Sam nodded sadly. He did not want any breakfast now, which was very unusual for Sam. He picked up his triangle and went out of the door.

Sam can never stay sad for long, because he has so many friends in Brand's Patch. As he rode through the village, he had so many people to wave to. Sad Gran and Granddad Bill were in their garden.

They called out, "Good Morning!" and, "See you later in the park!"

Sam could not help laughing as their bad cat Tom tipped over a bucket of weeds. This made Gran sad again!

After ten minutes of huffing and puffing on his bent, blue bike, and waving to anybody he saw, Sam arrived at the band room.

62

The band room is on the edge of the park, and Sam was very out of breath. His friends were there already and they looked very pleased to see him. There was PC Jack with his trumpet, and Bernard the Bandmaster holding his conductor's stick.

In the corner stood a tall, thin man with a very nice tan and a very smart suit on. He didn't look pleased to see Sam at all.

"Hello Jim," said Sam nervously, "How was your holiday?"

Jim ignored his question, and just said "I suppose you found your clothes at a jumble sale, Sam?" Sam went purple and looked at his shoes, which were very scruffy indeed.

Before Sam had a chance to reply, Bernard stepped in. Glaring at Jim, who was now busy filing his nails, he said, "I'm glad you've come Sam. We were worried you might oversleep and not make it to the rehearsal."

"But I only play the triangle," said Sam, "It's not very important and no-one will hear if I make a mistake."

Bernard looked at Sam and said sternly, "Every instrument is important Sam, but that is not the reason we need you here."

Sam looked puzzled. Then suddenly something caught his eye. He turned his head and saw Jim polishing a bright, shiny long instrument with a big slide. It was a trombone! He turned back to face Bernard, his mind racing. If Jim was playing the trombone, he wouldn't be able to play the drum. Could it be that . . . ? No, he must try not to get excited.

Every time he had felt happy that morning, someone had made him sad. First Sue, then Jim, and now it looked like it would be Bernard.

But he had guessed Sam's thoughts, and beamed at him. His big rosy face was split by a huge grin.

"Jim has bought himself a present – a new trombone which he will play on the march this afternoon. So we need someone else to play the big drum."

Sam bit his lip, not daring to hope. Behind his back, he crossed every finger, and in his shoes, every toe was crossed.

"Sam, I would like you to play the drum this afternoon," Bernard told him.

Sam gasped and clapped his hands. He shouted for joy and everyone except Jim cheered and slapped Sam on the back. Sam had never felt so happy in his life. He would play the drum that afternoon, and everyone in Brand's Patch would look at him. He would bang as loudly as he could, which is very loud indeed!

The band all sat down in their places and began to tune their instruments. Sam proudly took his new place with the drum, and the rehearsal began.

They started with their favourite tune, the Brand's Patch Marching Song. They always played very well indeed, but today something was wrong.

Jim put the trombone to his lips, and began to push the slide up and down. His cheeks blew out, he went red in the face and some loud and rather strange noises came from the trombone. Everybody stopped playing and looked at Jim.

"Ahem," said Bernard, "Jim, can you actually play that trombone?"

"Of course I can play it," snapped Jim, who was as red as his big car, "I would not have bought it, if I could not play it, would I?"

Jim looked accusingly at Bernard, his eyes flashing and his

lips thin and set. Bernard looked at Jim and decided not to argue!

"Right, play on! Trombone section, keep it down please!" Bernard tapped his stick and everyone had to hide their smiles as Jim made the strangest noises they had ever heard.

Sam happily played the drum as loudly as he could, giggling quietly to himself every time a strange and rather rude noise came out of the end of Jim's trombone.

Bang, Bang, Bang, went the drum,
Bang-Bang, Bang-Bang
Bang, Bang, Bang
Wa, wa-wa-wa. WA-WA, went the trombone.

Sam giggled again and kept banging, until Bernard said that he was happy and the rehearsal was over.

"Right then everyone," said Bernard looking at his watch. "It's 2 o'clock, nearly time to set off for the park. Everyone will be there, so we must play our best and look very smart in our white shirts."

Bernard looked very hard at Sam when he said this, and Sam hastily tucked in his shirt, which, with all his banging had fallen out of his trousers.

"Right," Bernard boomed again. "Everybody outside. Get ready to march to the park!"

Everyone picked up their instruments excitedly, and some began combing their hair and spitting on their shoes to make them shine.

Sam picked up the big drum and walked out with PC Jack, who was carrying his trumpet.

When everybody was outside, Bernard began to position the band in the correct order. Sam looked at Jim, who was proudly showing off the slide of his new trombone to a group of boys who had gathered to see the band off.

"I wouldn't like to be marching in front of Jim," thought Sam. "That slide looks awfully good for poking people in the back with!"

Soon nearly everybody was in order, and only Sam and Jim were left.

"Sam, you will march next so go and stand behind PC Jack please, and keep everybody in time." Sam walked over to PC Jack, with the drum strapped across his shoulders.

"Alright," said Bernard, 'I think we're ready to go!"

"Err, not quite ready Bernard," sneered Jim, who still had not been given his place.

Bernard looked round and saw Jim standing alone with his trombone. The truth was, Bernard had not forgotten Jim at all, he just did not want him to play in the band because of the awful noise Jim made on his trombone.

"Ah yes, Jim, you will march at the end, behind Sam, if you don't mind," said Bernard, looking cross. Sam groaned as Jim walked over, pushing and pulling his slide in and out and grinning nastily.

"Oh no, I don't mind marching behind Sam one little bit," he said. Sam gulped and tried to concentrate on his drum. "Heads up everyone, look sharp and good luck. Bang the drum Sam, and then we will start to play."

Sam's chest swelled with pride as he lifted his sticks to start the band marching.

Bang, Bang, Bang
Bang-Bang, Bang-Bang

Bang, Bang, Bang

Sadly he knew that Jim with his silver trombone was marching just behind him.

Wa-wa-wa-wa. WA WA WA

The loud noises came out and it was hard for Sam to hear the tune the band was playing. But he marched on, banging the drum.

As they got close to the edge of the park, Sam could hear the cheers of everybody gathered to watch the marching band. He felt so excited and banged the drum extra loud. Sam could pick out faces he knew in the crowd – Sad Gran and Granddad Bill were there. So was Sue, who looked very smart indeed. Even Sam's sister Flossie, who had come on the train from her house in Fling, just to see the band! How surprised they would all be to see Sam playing the drum!

All the boys and girls from the village school had the afternoon off to watch the band, and they were dancing and shouting with excitement. Some were on the swings, flying high to get a better view of the band.

Sam felt so happy and so proud – he did not think he had ever been so happy in his whole life, when suddenly, he felt a dig in the back. Then – another one.

"What's that?" he thought.

Dig-Dig-Dig. Dig-Dig – he felt in his back.

Wa-wa-wa. WA WA – he heard with his ears.

The jolting was pushing him off his stride. They were getting closer and closer to the waiting crowd, and Sam could not play his drum properly! He was going to look a fool in front of Sue, Sad Gran, Granddad Bill, and Flossie!

Dig-Dig

Wa-wa

Ouch! Ouch!

Dig-Dig

Wa-wa

Ouch! Ouch!

Bang Bang

Dig-Dig

Wa-wa

"OUCH! OUCH!" shouted Sam, banging his drum all out of time.

Without the drum to keep them in time, the band started to play all wrong, and they were nearly at the waiting crowd.

"What's the matter with you Sam?" hissed PC Jack.

"It's Jim!" spluttered Sam., "He keeps OUCH poking me in the back."

"What's going on back there!" Bernard shouted, desperately trying to keep the band together. Sam tried to shout back, but Jim gave him an extra large poke and he could not get the words out!

Dig-Dig

Wa-Wa

Ouch-Ouch!

PC Jack turned round to try to stop Jim, who was poking so hard he was making the most awful sounds. Sam did not see Jack turn in time and as he raised his drumstick to hit as hard as he could, Jim delivered his hardest poke yet.

Sam fell forward, hitting PC Jack hard on the head. The band was alongside the crowd now, who could see what was happening and were clutching their sides with laughter and pointing at Sam and his drum.

Sam had wanted every one to look at him playing the drum, but this was not quite what he had had in mind! He could see Sue standing with her hands on her hips, looking furious. Sad Gran looking sadder than ever. Flossie was waving her hands for help, but Jim just carried on poking and laughing.

Sam has many friends, especially amongst the boys and girls in the village who love the special sweets and cakes he makes in his kitchen. They had seen from the swings that Jim was spoiling the march, and had run over as fast as they could. The children reached the band and shouted to Jim.

"Stop that. Stop that. You are hurting his back, and spoiling the day for everyone. STOP IT!"

The band stopped marching – some of the boys and girls stood in the way. Bernard turned to them, red with rage and embarrassment.

"Get out of the way," he shouted, "we must march on!"

"No," they said. "We will not go until you tell Jim to stop digging Sam in the back with his trombone. He is stopping Sam from playing and ruining the march."

Silence fell over the crowd and all eyes turned to Jim, who was trying to look innocent, and Sam, who was out of breath and hurting all over.

"Is this true?" Bernard asked Sam.

"Yes – Yes – it really hurts. I bet I've got lots of bruises," he groaned.

Bernard turned to Jim with such a look of fury on his face that Jim shrank back.

"I knew that trombone would be trouble the moment I saw it. You have hurt Sam and you have ruined the most important day of the year for the Brand's Patch Band. I hope you're ashamed of yourself. Take your trombone back to your big house and don't come back until you want to be a true band member."

Everyone in the crowd glared at Jim and the nasty smile was wiped off his face. He stuck his long, thin nose in the air, turned on his heel and stomped off in the direction of his big house. He only stopped to throw his brand new trombone into the park bin.

Bernard turned to Sam and said, "I am sorry your big moment has been spoiled. I know how excited you were about playing the drum, and now Jim has ruined everything."

"No he hasn't!" piped up a small voice. Everyone turned to look, and there was one of the boys, holding Jim's trombone in his hand. "I can play the trombone, and now I have the brand new one. Let me play the trombone part, and march on with the band."

"What a great idea," said Bernard, "What's your name boy?"

"My name is Ali," said the boy.

"Well Ali, I think you and Sam should stand right at the front and we should march a lap of honour all the way around the park, and right past Jim's front door!" said Bernard.

A loud cheer went up from the crowd, and Sam and Ali beamed. Bernard turned to the rest of the children and said, "You can march along behind if you like."

So the band set off again, and Ali turned out to be a very good trombone player. As for Sam, he hit his drum louder than ever, keeping the band perfectly in time. When everyone turned to look, it was for all the right reasons!